▲ Lake Buttermere (Lake District)

raintree

Raintree is an imprint of Capstone Global Library Limited, a company incorporated in England and Wales having its registered office at 264 Banbury Road, Oxford, OX2 7DY – Registered company number: 6695582

www.raintree.co.uk
myorders@raintree.co.uk

Edited by Helen Cox Cannons
Designed by Ted Williams and Kazuko Collins
Original illustrations © Capstone Global Library Limited 2018
Illustrated by Eric Gohl
Picture research by Jo Miller
Production by Kathy McColley
Originated by Capstone Global Library Ltd
Printed and bound in India

ISBN 978 1 4747 5397 5 (hardcover)
21 20 19 18 17
10 9 8 7 6 5 4 3 2 1

ISBN 978 1 4747 5399 9 (paperback)
22 21 20 19
10 9 8 7 6 5 4 3 2

British Library Cataloguing in Publication Data
A full catalogue record for this book is available from the British Library.

Acknowledgements
We would like to thank the following for permission to reproduce photographs:

Image Credits
Alamy: Andrew Ray, 17, Dean Hoskins, 18, Nature Photographers Ltd, 13, Wild Places Photography/Chris Howes, 31; Capstone: Eric Gohl, throughout, (detail maps); Fotolia: nspooner, 26; iStockphoto: Ianwool, 23; Shutterstock: Billy Stock, 2, Brendan Howard, 33, 48, chris2766, 3, (middle), 28, CKP1001, 16, (top), Dave Carroll, 22, Dave Head, 20, davemhuntphotography, 37, David Hughes, 6, DavidYoung, 11, gubenat, 45, Helen Hotson, 10, Jamie Hall, 7, Jane Rix, 3, (top), JPagetRFPhotos, back cover, (top), JuliusKielaitis, 1, Lance Bellers, 29, Lukasz Pajor, 9, 24, Malago, 35, back cover, (background), Mark A. Rice, 25, Mark Bulmer, 30, Mark Medcalf, 32, Martin Fowler, 12, Martin Prochazkacz, 16, (bottom), Mike Charles, 4, (top), Mirko Graul, 8, Miroslav Hlavko, 39, Philip Birtwistle, 14, Pinkcandy, 3, (bottom), Rainer Lesniewski, 5, throughout, (location map), Ramon Harkema, 40, 42, Robert Trevis-Smith, 21, Ross Elliott Photo, 36, Spumador, 41, Stefano Zaccaria, 43, Stewart Smith Photography, cover, stocker1970, 38, 44, Stockimo, 27, travelight, 47, Traveller70, 34, Valdis Skudre, 4, (bottom); Wikimedia: Ian Stannard, 19

Design Elements
Shutterstock: Dave Carroll, Flas100

CONTENTS

Some words are shown in **bold**, like this. You can find out
what they mean by looking in the glossary.

▲ Cairngorms

▲ Seven Sisters Cliffs
(South Downs)

▲ Loch Lomond

WELCOME TO THE UK'S NATIONAL PARKS!

The UK has a huge variety of landscapes, **geology**, history, wildlife and natural beauty. The National Parks were created to protect and **preserve** the most special of these areas. Today, there are 15 National Parks in the UK – 10 in England, 2 in Scotland and 3 in Wales. No two parks are the same and there are plenty of opportunities to try out fun activities during a visit, from snowboarding in the Cairngorms to seashore safaris in Exmoor! There are currently no National Parks in Northern Ireland, but the country has many **Areas of Outstanding Natural Beauty**.

Each park is looked after by its own organization, but the larger organization called National Parks UK is in charge of the entire park system. These organizations work hard to care for the land within the parks. They run many important **conservation** projects to protect threatened wildlife and their habitats. It is also the job of National Parks UK to help protect communities inside the parks, while making sure the parks are safe for millions of visitors.

Stanage Edge (Peak District) ▶

1 The Broads Population: 6,271; **Visitors per year:** 8 million; **Area:** 303 square kilometres

2 Dartmoor Population: 34,000; **Visitors per year:** 2.4 million; **Area:** 953 square kilometres

3 Exmoor Population: 10,600; **Visitors per year:** 1.4 million; **Area:** 694 square kilometres

4 The Lake District Population: 41,100; **Visitors per year:** 16.4 million; **Area:** 2,362 square kilometres

5 The New Forest Population: 34,922; **Visitors per year:** Not available; **Area:** 570 square kilometres

6 Northumberland Population: 2,200; **Visitors per year:** 1.5 million; **Area:** 1,048 square kilometres

7 The North York Moors Population: 23,380; **Visitors per year:** 7 million; **Area:** 1,434 square kilometres

8 The Peak District Population: 37,905; **Visitors per year:** 8.75 million; **Area:** 1,437 square kilometres

9 The South Downs Population: 120,00; **Visitors per year:** Not available; **Area:** 1,624 square kilometres

10 The Yorkshire Dales Population: 23,637; **Visitors per year:** 9.5 million; **Area:** 2,178 square kilometres

11 The Cairngorms Population: 17,000; **Visitors per year:** 1.5 million; **Area:** 4,528 square kilometres

12 Loch Lomond & The Trossachs Population: 15,600; **Visitors per year:** 4 million; **Area:** 1,865 square kilometres

13 The Brecon Beacons Population: 32,000; **Visitors per year:** 4.15 million; **Area:** 1,344 square kilometres

14 The Pembrokeshire Coast Population: 22,800; **Visitors per year:** 4.2 million; **Area:** 621 square kilometres

15 Snowdonia Population: 25,482; **Visitors per year:** 4.27 million; **Area:** 2,176 square kilometres

Worstead

Hickling Broad

River Bure

THE BROADS NATIONAL PARK

Norwich

Breydon Water Great Yarmouth

River Yare

N
W · E
S

English Channel

▲ One of the best ways to experience the Broads' peaceful waterways is by boat.

The Broads National Park is the UK's largest protected **wetland**. This makes it the perfect habitat for water-loving birds, such as bitterns, terns and the common crane. Insects and mammals love the wetlands too. Dragonflies and butterflies hover in the marshes, while water voles and otters make their homes in the **reed beds**.

Landscape

The Broads is famous for its "lakes" (known as broads), rivers and streams. Many of these waterways are connected, so people can travel by boat, canoe or kayak all over the park. Most of these waterways were formed by accident. At the start of the **Iron Age** (around 800 BC), the land in the Broads was mainly marshes and **peat** bogs. During the Middle Ages (12th–14th centuries), the people living in this area dug up millions of tonnes of peat to sell as fuel. This left many huge, deep pits. The land in the Broads is very low-lying. When sea levels rose, the seawater flooded the pits. This created the broads and waterways we see in the park today.

Activities

There are around 200 kilometres of waterways in the Broads. This makes it the perfect park for watersports! Many people come here to go on a cruise boat or explore hidden streams on a kayak or paddleboard. But there is

With their brown feathers, bitterns are difficult to spot among the reed beds. But you may be able to hear their strange, booming call!

more to the Broads than just watersports. There are around 300 kilometres of great cycle paths and nature trails in this park's beautiful countryside.

History

The Broads isn't only known for its waterways – in fact, this National Park is the only park to include a major city (Norwich). There are also lots of historic villages and market towns to explore. During the 1100s, weavers from Flanders (part of Belgium) arrived to settle in the village of Worstead. They brought with them knowledge and skills for weaving cloth by hand. Worstead cloth was made from sheep's wool. It quickly became famous, and was sold all over the country. To celebrate their success, the weavers built St Mary's Church in the village, which is still open to visitors and worshippers.

-Symbol of the Broads-

The Broads Authority looks after the Broads National Park. Its logo is the Norfolk hawker dragonfly. This is because almost all of these rare dragonflies in the UK are found in the Broads. But this rare insect and its habitat are under threat. Many marshes have been cleared to create farmland for cattle to graze on. **Pollution** also seeps into the marsh water from nearby towns and villages. Park staff and volunteers have been working hard to change this. Nature reserves are protected by law, so the park's dragonfly experts have built several new dragonfly habitat sites within these reserves. Thanks to this work, the Norfolk hawker has a much brighter future.

The Broads' many windmills were once used for grinding corn and draining flooded marshes.

The stone circle and stone row at Down Tor are among Dartmoor's most impressive Bronze Age features.

Dartmoor is the biggest and wildest open area of countryside in southern England. It is famous for its dramatic moorland and its rocky peaks, known as tors. But the park also has a mysterious history.

Landscape

Tors are rock peaks that jut out of the ground. Most tors are formed of a hard rock called granite. Millions of years ago, the granite rock lay beneath the ground. But over time, rain, wind and rivers washed the ground away, leaving the granite peaks behind. There are hundreds of tors in Dartmoor. Some, like Great Mis Tor, are tall, mountain-like peaks. Others, like Flat Tor, are small and almost flat.

History

During the early **Bronze Age**, the people of Dartmoor built stone circles and rows. The rows are a series of huge rocks placed in straight lines up to 200 metres long. Archaeologists and historians think stone rows were used for ceremonies or built as tributes to the dead. There are around 75 stone rows still standing in Dartmoor. The most impressive of these is Stalldown Stone Row, which is 500 metres long!

Activities

Did you know that Dartmoor is the only national park in England to allow wild camping? Wild camping is different from staying in a campsite – there are no toilets, shops or campsite attendants. Instead, wild campers can set up their tents almost anywhere in the park! Wild campers carry all their equipment in a backpack and take everything away again, including rubbish and waste. They leave the place as they found it, so that others can enjoy it in the future.

-Dartmoor's- famous pony

The Dartmoor pony is a small, hardy breed. It lives on the moors, and is able to survive the strong winds and lack of shelter. But Dartmoor ponies are not wild animals. They are owned by farmers and pony **herders**, who release the ponies to graze the moors for most of the year. The ponies eat vegetation that other livestock cannot, including gorse, brambles and bracken. This stops these plants from spreading and taking over. In turn, this allows lots of plant and flower species to survive on the moors.

▲ Dartmoor ponies rest at Birch Tor.

11

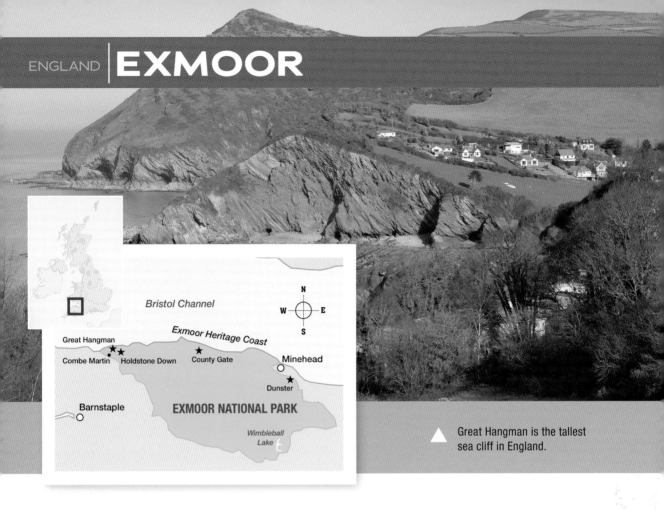

Bristol Channel

Exmoor Heritage Coast

Great Hangman
Combe Martin   Holdstone Down   County Gate
Minehead
Dunster
Barnstaple
EXMOOR NATIONAL PARK
Wimbleball Lake

N
W — E
S

Great Hangman is the tallest sea cliff in England.

With only 10,600 people living in Exmoor, this park can feel wild and remote. But there is plenty to see and do here, from taking part in seashore safaris to spotting one of the UK's rarest trees.

Landscape

Exmoor is famous for its Heritage Coast, which has some of the tallest cliffs in the UK. Great Hangman, at Combe Martin, is England's highest sea cliff. The cliff face drops 244 metres to the sea below! Be sure to listen for nesting seabirds, such as guillemots and razorbills, and keep an eye out for the wild Exmoor ponies and mountain goats that roam the hillside.

Activity

Dunster and Combe Martin are great beaches for rockpooling. Marine wildlife, such as starfish, crabs and sea anemones, live on these shores. Visitors can join a guided seashore safari and examine their finds under a microscope.

Nature

Exmoor has around 25 square kilometres of ancient woodland. Over thousands of years, people living here cut down trees to use for firewood and building houses. But today cutting is closely managed, so that these ancient woodlands are protected for future **generations**. The Exmoor woodlands are famous for three species of whitebeam trees. They do not grow anywhere else in the world and are very rare in the wild. Whitebeams grow on rocky slopes and along footpaths.

You can spot them by their clusters of five-petalled flowers, which bloom in early summer. The flowers develop into coloured berries in autumn.

Several species of whitebeam tree are native to Exmoor. This means they can't be found anywhere else in the world.

13

THE LAKE DISTRICT NATIONAL PARK

Bassenthwaite Lake
Keswick
Ullswater
Helvellyn
Scafell Pike
Windermere
Hill Top Farm
Kendal
Irish Sea

At 14.8 square kilometres, Windermere is England's largest natural lake. It is also the most famous lake in the park.

At 2,362 square kilometres, the Lake District is England's largest National Park. It is also the busiest National Park in the UK, with 16.4 million visitors a year! In 2017, the Lake District became a **UNESCO World Heritage Site**. Other UNESCO sites around the world include the Grand Canyon in Arizona, USA, the Taj Mahal in India and the Sydney Opera House in Australia.

Landscape

You are never far from a beautiful lake in this park! There are 16 big lakes and many smaller lakes to choose from. The big lakes are known as "waters" or "meres". The smaller lakes are called "tarns" (the Old Norse word for mountain "pond" or "pool"). Many are ribbon lakes. They get their name because they are long and narrow, like a ribbon. These lakes were formed 13,000 years ago during the last ice age. Huge **glaciers** moved across the land, carving deep valleys. As the glaciers melted, the valleys were filled with meltwater and rainwater. This created the lakes we see today.

Fells are tall, flat mountains and hills. They are usually bare on top, with very few trees. There are at least 200 fells in the Lake District, one of which is England's highest mountain, Scafell Pike (978 metres). "Fellbaggers" are people who return to the park every year to climb as many different fells as possible. Look closely, and you may also see fell runners racing up and down the hillsides!

-Beatrix Potter-

Hill Top Farm, in Near Sawrey, was the home of world-famous children's author Beatrix Potter (1866–1943). The Lake District's wildlife inspired Beatrix's much-loved characters, such as Peter Rabbit, Jemima Puddle-Duck and Mrs Tiggywinkle. Beatrix was also an **environmentalist** – she saved 15 farms and their land from destruction. When she died in 1943, she left most of this land to the Lake District National Park.

No trip to the Lake District is complete without a lake cruise! *The Lady of the Lake* is thought to be the oldest working passenger ferry in the world. It ferries passengers across beautiful Ullswater. On the journey, keep an eye out for Helvellyn, one of the highest fells in the park (950 metres).

-Kendal Mint Cake-

Kendal Mint Cake is a peppermint-flavoured sugary snack. It has been made in the village of Kendal for 100 years. It is popular with hikers and climbers, as the sugar gives them energy to tackle the Lake District's steep fells.

-The Lake District Osprey Project-

Ospreys are fish-eating birds of prey. They were once a common sight across the UK. But during the 1800s, egg collectors raided osprey nests and hunted the adults. Their numbers quickly dropped. In the late 1990s, the staff of the Lake District Osprey Project built a nesting platform near Bassenthwaite Lake. They hoped that ospreys from Europe would move in and breed. In 2001, an osprey pair finally nested on the platform and bred a chick – the first to be born in the Lake District in 150 years. Volunteers have since built more platforms and ospreys return to breed each year.

▲ Ullswater Lake is the second-largest lake in England. Its stunning mountain scenery includes a view of Helvellyn.

THE NEW FOREST NATIONAL PARK

Southampton

Lyndhurst

Yew Tree Heath

Beaulieu

The Solent

Bournemouth

Milford on Sea

Hurst Castle

If you're lucky, you may get a chance to spot wild sika deer roaming the New Forest woodland.

The New Forest is actually very old! In 1079, King William I (1028–1087) turned these woods into a royal hunting ground. He and his men hunted wild deer and boar. Only royalty and the richest people in the land were allowed to hunt in the New Forest. But poorer people had the right to graze their cattle, pigs and ponies in the forest. This was known as "Commoners rights". This right has been passed down the generations, and New Forest ponies, cattle and pigs still roam the woods today. There are also five species of deer in the forest – red, roe, fallow, sika and muntjac.

History

You might see low, rounded hills dotted around the New Forest. These are ancient burial mounds, or barrows. They were positioned on a ridge so that tribe members could easily see them and remember the dead. Experts have dated the barrows back to the early-middle Bronze Age. You can see several Bronze Age barrows at Yew Tree Heath, near the village of Beaulieu.

Castles

Hurst Castle is a huge fortress at the end of a long **spit** of land near Milford-on-Sea, across the water from the Isle of Wight. King Henry VIII (1491–1597) built the castle to defend the south coast from French invaders. It had a **keep** and **ramparts**, with around 20 guns and hundreds of soldiers. In the 1870s, long armoured wings were added to the original castle. Powerful 38-tonne guns were set up in the armoured wings. You can still see two of these guns

▲ Hurst Castle

at the castle today. Hurst Castle is no longer used as a fortress, but it is open to tourists between April and October. To get there, visitors can catch a ferry from Keyhaven or walk along the spit at low tide.

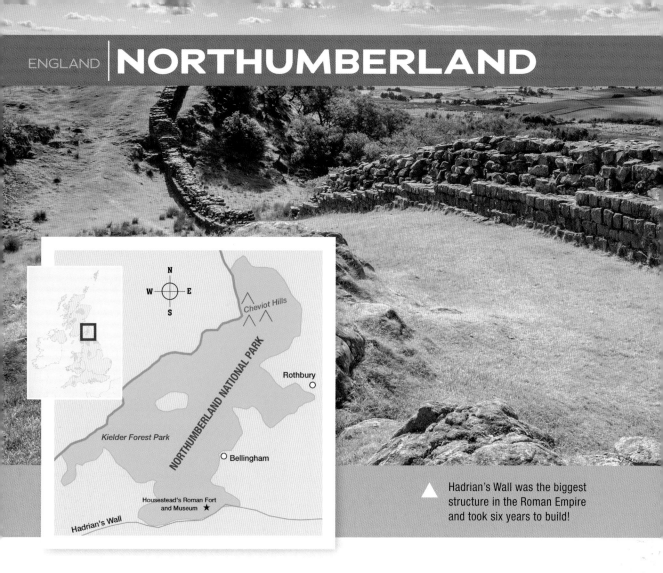

Hadrian's Wall was the biggest structure in the Roman Empire and took six years to build!

Northumberland National Park is in the north of England, on the border with Scotland. It is the least populated of the UK's National Parks, as only 2,000 people live here. However, 1.5 million visitors arrive here every year to learn about its fascinating history.

History

From AD 43 to AD 410, Britain, all except Scotland, was part of the Roman Empire. Emperor Hadrian (AD 76–AD 138) wanted to control his lands and protect Britannia from the **Picts**. He ordered his army to build a huge stone wall near the border with Caledonia (now Scotland). The wall ran for 117.5 kilometres, from the North Sea in the east to the Irish Sea in the west. It was 6 metres wide and 3.5 metres high in places. Today, visitors can walk the Hadrian's Wall Path. You can see some of Britain's best Roman fort ruins at the Roman Fort and Museum at Housesteads.

Landscape

The Cheviot Hills are beautiful rolling hills in the north of the park. They also stretch across the border into Scotland. These hills formed from lava flows, which are boiling hot rivers of rock. Between 460 and 360 million years, lava burst up from beneath the Earth's surface and flowed across the landscape. Eventually, these hot rivers stopped moving and hardened to form **igneous rock**. Grass slowly grew over the rock, creating hills and valleys. Today, there are lots of pretty footpaths and trails all over the Cheviot Hills.

-The large- heath butterfly

The large heath butterfly lives near wet, boggy areas. Here, its caterpillars can feed on hare's tail cotton grass and the adult butterflies sip nectar from other bog plants. In the 20th century, many bogs were drained to make way for industry and farmland. The large heath butterfly's numbers dropped across the UK. Today, conservation groups are working hard to protect large heath **colonies**. In Kielder Forest, staff and volunteers have cleared trees to make more bog habitat. The large heath butterfly now returns to the park year after year.

THE NORTH YORK MOORS

The rocky shores of the North York Moors' "Dinosaur Coast" are rich in ancient fossils and rare dinosaur bones.

The North York Moors is the largest area of heather moorland in the UK. There are very few trees. Instead, fields of heather grow low to the ground. This is the perfect habitat for many small mammals and ground-nesting birds. But, millions of years ago, dinosaurs also roamed this land.

Landscape

The North York Moors coast dates back to the Jurassic period (150–200 million years ago). This is why it's sometimes called the "Dinosaur Coast". **Paleontologists** have discovered thousands of rare dinosaur bones, ammonite fossils and even dinosaur footprints in these rocks! Today, visitors can join a fossil hunting trip at Saltwick Bay.

Wildlife

Wykeham Forest is home to the merlin falcon, the UK's smallest bird of prey. The merlin is an expert flyer and skilled hunter. It hovers then dives into heather to catch its prey, such as sparrows and quail. But the merlin is a threatened species. Only 1,300 pairs remain in the UK, of which 40 are in the park. The North York Moors was made a **Special Protection Area** to protect the merlins' habitat and give them a safe place to hunt and breed.

-Baytown's- smugglers

During the late 1700s, the tiny fishing village of Robin Hood's Bay, then called Baytown, became one of Britain's busiest smuggling communities. Mighty ships from overseas brought goods to the shore. The smugglers hid the goods in alleyways, beach coves and pub basements, before selling them in secret on the **black market** to avoid paying government taxes. Visitors to "Baytown" can join a guided tour to learn more about the smugglers and their risky work.

THE PEAK DISTRICT

THE PEAK DISTRICT
NATIONAL PARK

Sheffield

Stanage Edge ★

Eyam ●

Bakewell ●

The Roaches ★

River Dove

Dovedale
Valley

Stoke-on-Trent ○

The Peak District is famous for its dark caves and deep valleys, such as Dovedale Valley in Derbyshire.

The Peak District, opened in 1951, was the UK's first National Park. It spreads over five counties: Cheshire, Derbyshire, Greater Manchester, West Yorkshire and South Yorkshire. It is also one of the most visited parks in the UK. People come to the park to enjoy its fascinating geology, tasty treats and deadly history...

Activity

As well as deep valleys and caves, the Peak District is known for its many tall cliffs. These cliffs feature some of the most challenging rock climbs in Europe. Stanage Edge, near Sheffield, is where the sport of rock climbing first began. People have been climbing this cliff since the 1800s. Beginners can try easier routes with a guide, while visitors who don't like heights can sit back and watch climbers testing their strength on the cliff face.

There are around 2,000 climbing routes at Stanage Edge, near Sheffield.

-Tasty treat-

A good place to stop for a sweet treat in the Peak District is Bakewell. Here you can try the famous Bakewell pudding, which has been made in the village since the early 1800s. You may have heard of the Bakewell tart, but the traditional Bakewell pudding has a completely different texture and taste. It has a flaky pastry base, a layer of jam and an egg and almond paste filling. Enjoy it hot or cold, with custard or cream!

History

The Peak District has many beautiful villages, but one village in Derbyshire has a deadly history. In 1665, the Great Plague swept through London. Bubonic plague was a deadly disease carried by fleas. In 1665, Eyam's village tailor received a parcel of cloth from London containing bubonic plague fleas. The tailor died within a week. To stop the disease spreading to the rest of north England, villagers cut themselves off from the outside world. They left money at boundary stones on the edge of the village in exchange for food and medicine. Around 260 out of 350 villagers ended up dying from plague. But they managed to stop the disease spreading beyond Eyam, which saved thousands of lives. Today, visitors can see one of the original boundary stones and the graves of the Riley family, while Eyam Museum tells the village's plague story.

-The Peak District millstone-

As you arrive at the Peak District, look out for a wheel-shaped rock on the roadside. These large, man-made rocks are known as millstones. Since the 1700s, people have made the wheel-shaped millstones from rocks there. Millers would grind grains such as wheat, oats and barley between two millstones to make flour. The millstone is now the Peak District National Park's symbol. When you pass one, you'll know that you're in the park!

PEAK NATIONAL PARK

▲ The Roaches, a rocky ridge near the town of Leek, Staffordshire, is popular with hikers and climbers.

THE SOUTH DOWNS

The Seven Sisters cliffs make up part of the 160-kilometre trail known as the South Downs Way.

The South Downs is a beautiful park, with chalky white cliffs and rolling green hills. It is also the UK's newest National Park, although it has an ancient history.

Landscape

Between 75 and 90 million years ago, a shallow tropical sea covered much of England. Over millions of years, thick layers of limestone rock formed at the bottom of this warm ocean. As the sea retreated, huge chalk cliffs and hills were revealed over time. These are known as the Seven Sisters, in East Sussex.

Activity

Geocaching is an exciting treasure hunt in the outdoors! Geocachers around the world use map coordinates to hide and seek containers, or "caches". Caches contain a pencil, a logbook and treasures such as small toys, unusual coins and books. The seeker records his find in the logbook and returns it to the cache. The South Downs runs a GeoTour of 30 geocaches.

History

On 5 November 1605, Guy Fawkes and other men plotted to blow up London's Houses of Parliament with gunpowder. On Bonfire Night, adults set off fireworks and light bonfires to remember the Gunpowder Plot. Every year on 5 November, the usually quiet town of Lewes erupts with the country's largest Bonfire Night festival.

-The Long Man- of Wilmington

If you're travelling near Wimington, East Sussex, you may spot a mysterious white figure carved into the white rock in a hillside. At 72 metres tall, the Long Man can be seen for many miles. People once thought that the Long Man was created during the Iron Age. But experts now say he probably dates from the 1500s or 1600s. During World War II (1939–1945), locals painted the white man green to match the grassy hillside, so that enemy planes flying overhead couldn't use him as a landmark.

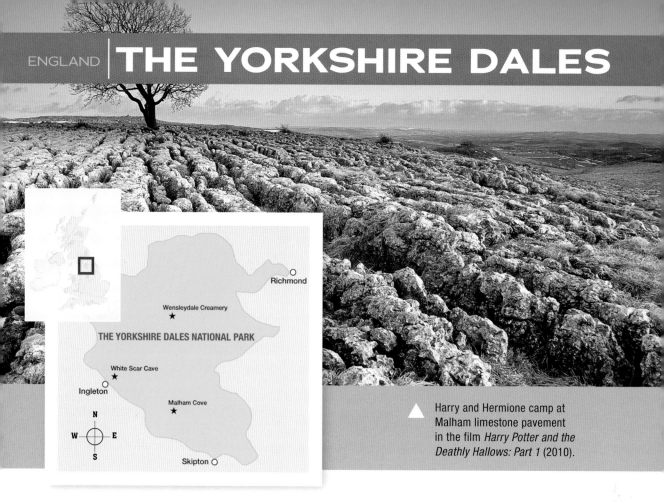

ENGLAND | THE YORKSHIRE DALES

Richmond

Wensleydale Creamery
★

THE YORKSHIRE DALES NATIONAL PARK

White Scar Cave
★
Ingleton

Malham Cove
★

N
W ─ E
S

Skipton

Harry and Hermione camp at Malham limestone pavement in the film *Harry Potter and the Deathly Hallows: Part 1* (2010).

From these deep caves to the rolling green valleys, or dales, this park is great for all explorers!

Landscape

The Yorkshire Dales has some of the best limestone caves in the UK. Malham Cove is an 80-metre high cliff face. Above the Cove is the UK's longest limestone "pavement". Millions of years ago, glaciers scraped away soil to reveal bare limestone rock. Rain **eroded** the limestone and created pavement-like cracks in its surface. Visitors can walk a footpath to see the cove. There are also steps leading up to the limestone pavement.

In the Three Counties Caves, stalagmites grow up from the floor and stalactites hang from the ceiling.

The Three Counties is the longest cave system in the UK. It has 86 kilometres of tunnels and is 253 metres deep. These caves were formed over million of years. Streams both above and underground washed over the limestone, eroding the rock over millions of years. This made grand caverns and narrow tunnels. Brave explorers can take guided tours to White Scar Cave to see underground waterfalls. There are also rock formations with strange names, such as The Witch's Fingers and The Devil's Head!

History

Drystone walls are a common sight in this park. There are more miles of drystone wall in Yorkshire than in any other county. Drystone walls are made without cement. Instead, the builder carefully balances rocks of different shapes and sizes on top of each other. They are surprisingly strong – some date back to Neolithic times (starting around 10,000 BC).

-Lovely- cheese, Gromit!

If you're a fan of the animated characters Wallace and Gromit, you'll know that Wallace is crackers about Wensleydale cheese! The Wensleydale Creamery in Hawes has been making this famous crumbly cheese for more than 100 years. You can watch cheesemakers work and try Wallace's favourite cheese yourself at the creamery's visitor centre.

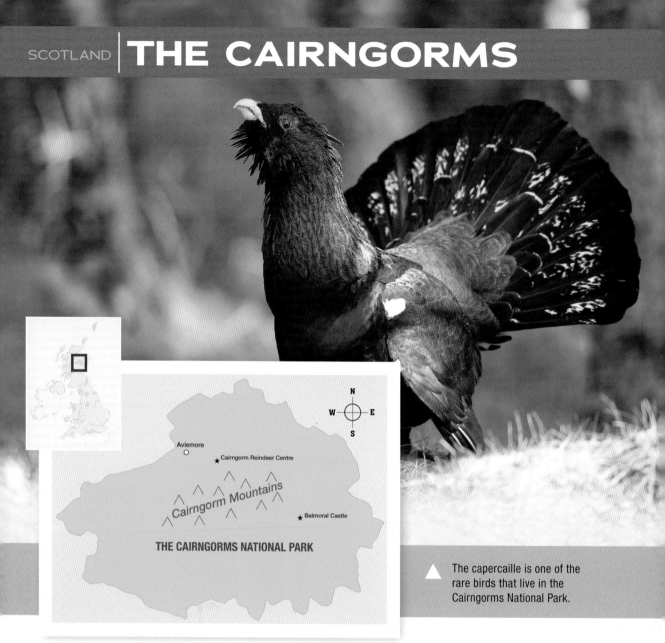

SCOTLAND | THE CAIRNGORMS

Aviemore

★ Cairngorm Reindeer Centre

Cairngorm Mountains

★ Balmoral Castle

THE CAIRNGORMS NATIONAL PARK

The capercaille is one of the rare birds that live in the Cairngorms National Park.

The Cairngorms is famous for its beautiful mountains. In fact, the park has five of Scotland's six highest peaks (Ben Nevis, the highest mountain in the UK at 1,345 metres, is outside the park). Some of these mountains are so tall that they get a lot of snow during winter. This makes the Cairngorms the perfect park for snowsports! Some of the UK's rarest wildlife also thrives in this winter wonderland.

Wildlife

The Cairngorms is the UK's biggest National Park. Its forests and mountains are home to 25 per cent of the UK's **endangered species** of animals. Rare mammals include the Scottish wildcat, red squirrel and mountain hare. There are also rare birds – golden eagles soar in the skies and capercaillies **forage** on the ground for food. But the Scottish crossbill is rarest of all. It is the only bird that lives nowhere else in the world but Scotland.

Activity

If you like winter sports, then you're in luck. The Cairngorms is one of the only places in the UK where you can ski, snowboard and cross-country ski outdoors. This is because there are more snow days here than anywhere else in the UK – around 76 a year! You can also ride the **Funicular** Mountain Railway to the top of Cairngorm Mountain between December and May.

-Travel in- luxury

The Caledonian Sleeper is no ordinary train. The service runs overnight between London and Scotland, and its passengers sleep in beds in their very own carriage. The journey between London and Aviemore in the park takes 10.5 hours.

▲ The Cairngorms is home to three of Scotland's five ski centres.

33

Castles

Balmoral Castle has been the Royal Family's Scottish holiday home since 1852, when Prince Albert (1819–1861) bought it for Queen Victoria (1819–1901). Since then, members of the Royal Family have spent many holidays at the castle. Today, the castle grounds and gardens are open to visitors, but not the rooms, as they are the Queen's private quarters.

Balmoral Castle's beautiful gardens and grounds are open to visitors during the summer months.

-Alpine animals-

Parts of the Cairngorms have an Arctic-alpine climate. Arctic-alpine regions are high up in mountains, where it is too cold for trees to survive. But reindeer really love this chilly weather. The UK's only free-ranging reindeer herd lives high up in the Cairngorms mountains. Free-ranging animals roam freely for at least part of the day, and the Cairngorms reindeer have a massive 10,000 acres to roam in. The staff at The Reindeer Company care for the reindeer. They also give guided walks up the mountain to the herd, where visitors get the chance to hand-feed these magnificent animals!

Reindeer are gentle animals with soft, velvety muzzles. This makes them a delight to hand-feed.

LOCH LOMOND & THE TROSSACHS

△ Ben More

LOCH LOMOND & THE TROSSACHS NATIONAL PARK

Inversnaid
Great Trossachs Forest
Callander

Tarbet

Loch Lomond

Luss
Inchcailloch/Loch Lomond
★ Nature Reserve

N
W E
S

Dumbarton

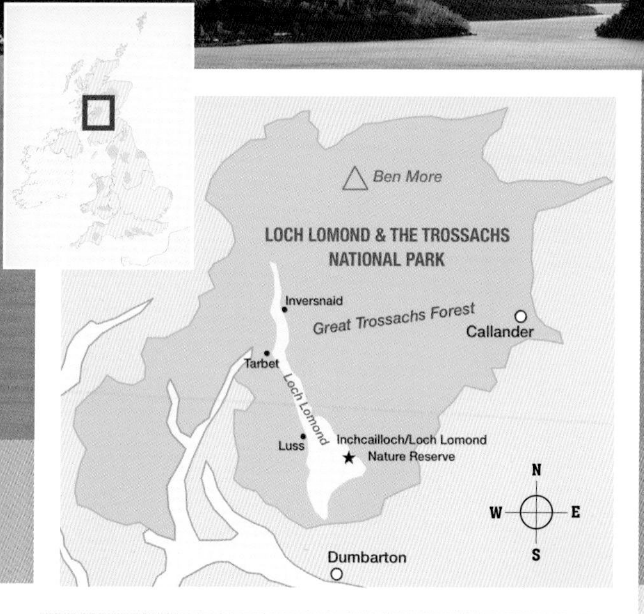

The shores of Loch Lomond offer spectacular views of Ben Lomond, one of Scotland's most popular munros.

From enormous lochs (Scottish lakes) to tall mountains to rare wildlife, there is something for everyone in Scotland's first National Park.

Landscape

This park is famous for its 22 large lochs and many smaller ones. The biggest of these is Loch Lomond (71 square kilometres). But look up and you'll also see the park's other best feature: its mountains.

In Scotland, mountains over 3,000 feet (or 914 metres) are known as munros. There are 283 munros in Scotland, 21 of which are in the park. Ben More is the highest, at 1,174 metres. "Munro baggers" are people who return to the park year after year to climb to the summit of every munro!

Activity

The best way to explore Loch Lomond is to hop aboard a boat cruise. Cruise Loch Lomond runs trips from several villages around the loch's coast, including Tarbet, Inversnaid and Luss. The boat also stops at the island of Inchcailloch, where you can visit the Loch Lomond Nature Reserve. Be sure to look for rare birdlife, including green and yellow wood warblers, pink-footed geese and ospreys. You may also see otters at the water's edge.

-The Scottish wildcat-

The Scottish wildcat may look just like a pet cat, but don't be fooled! This cat is a "super" predator with very sharp claws, strong jaws and fast reactions. A thick coat protects it from the cold Scottish winter. Its long, ringed tail helps it balance while it hunts rabbits, hares and mice. Sadly, the Scottish wildcat is close to **extinction**, as there are only around 100 left in the wild. Wildcats often breed with stray pet cats. This makes "hybrids", which are a mix of wildcats and pet cats. To stop this, experts in the park breed healthy wildcats in captivity, away from pet cats. They then release them into the Great Trossachs forest. The true wildcats then breed together, and their population grows.

THE BRECON BEACONS
WALES

The stunning Sgwd y Pannwr is one of four large waterfalls on the River Mellte, in the Brecon Beacons.

There is so much to do in the Brecon Beacons. One day you could be climbing a mountain, the next walking through a forest full of waterfalls!

Landscape

Coed-y-Rhaeadr ("Wood of the Water") is a forest filled with waterfalls. The Four Falls trail leads to Sgwd-y-Eira ("the Snow Waterfall"). Here, you can walk a path that takes you behind this tall waterfall. Visitors should keep to marked footpaths to avoid damaging the mosses, ferns and **lichens** that grow there. Near Coelbrehn, Henryhd Waterfall is the highest waterfall in the park. It has a drop of 27 metres – that's almost the height of a ten-storey building!

Geology

UNESCO Global GeoParks protect huge areas of unique and special geology. There are 127 GeoParks around the world. The Fforest Fawr ("Great Forest") is one of only seven in the UK. This GeoPark is 760 square kilometres and makes up the western half of Brecon Beacons National Park. It was named a GeoPark because of its unique rock formations. These include huge **sandstone** hills and limestone caves and pavements. The GeoPark also has the tallest mountain in the southern UK, Pen Y Fan (886 metres).

History

Drovers were hardy men who led herds of sheep, geese and other livestock across the Welsh mountains to markets in England. You can still walk some of the old drover roads in the park. One drover's road forms part of the Taff Trail. It starts at the Storey Arms Outdoor Education Centre.

-The tiny dormouse-

At only 6–9 centimetres long, the dormouse is one of the UK's tiniest mammals. Dormice nest in hedgerows or tree holes. They are only active at night, when they forage for nuts, seeds, berries and insects. But dormice are at risk. Loss of habitat and **climate change** threaten dormice food sources. Because of these threats, dormice are now protected by law. In Pwll y Wrach Nature Reserve, experts have been improving dormouse habitat by cutting back overgrown forest. This helps more light get to food that grows near the forest floor. With more food and better shelter, this tiny mammal should make a huge comeback!

Poppit Sands

Castell Henllys

St Davids

Ramsey Island   Newgale Beach

THE PEMBROKESHIRE COAST NATIONAL PARK

Skomer Island

Milford Haven

Dale Beach

N
W — E
S

Tenby

Caldey Island

Around 500 to 700 seal pups are born each year on Pembrokeshire's Ramsey Island.

The Pembrokeshire Coast, in south-west Wales, is the UK's only fully coastal National Park. Nowhere in the park is more than 16 kilometres away from the sea.

Wildlife

The Pembrokeshire Coast is one of the best places in Europe to see marine wildlife. Seabirds, grey seals, dolphins, and even orcas and basking sharks make their homes in these waters throughout the year.

Female grey seals come ashore to pup in autumn. Be sure to pack your binoculars if you want to see them, as visitors are forbidden from walking on beaches where there are seal pups.

Activity

There is no better way to explore the Pembrokeshire coast than to see it up close. Coasteering is an exciting adventure sport in which you get to clamber over coastal rocks, jump off sea cliffs and wave hop. This sport can be dangerous, so never try it alone or without an adult. There are several qualified guides in Pembrokeshire and everyone taking part must wear proper safety helmets and wetsuits. Anyone over the age of eight can join in the fun.

-Blue Flag beaches-

The Blue Flag is a special award given to the cleanest, safest beaches and marinas in the world. Pembrokeshire has more Blue Flag beaches per mile than anywhere else in the UK. Blue Flag beaches such as Dale, Poppit Sands and Newgale Sands are the perfect place for a picnic, a paddle in the sea or a day building sandcastles!

NEWGALE

Landscape

There are six small islands off the coast of Pembrokeshire. They are Ramsey, Caldey, Skomer, St Margaret's, Skokholm and Grassholm. Sailors from Norway and Denmark gave these islands their strange names – they used them as navigation markers when sailing in the Irish Sea. Today, all of these islands are part of the National Park. People still live on Caldey, but the other islands are nature reserves.

Visitors can take a boat trip to the reserves to see huge colonies of sea birds, such as puffins, guillemots and razorbills.

Puffins lay only one egg a year. Both parents take turns in keeping the egg warm and caring for the chick when it hatches.

History

If you want to see living, breathing history in Pembrokeshire, then head to Castell Henllys. The people of the Demetae tribe lived in this Iron Age Hill Fort around 2,000 years ago. The same breed of pigs that lived there during the Iron Age graze in the grounds today, and there are four **reconstructed** roundhouses to explore. Visitors can also train as warriors, listen to tales around a fire and meet Iron Age "villagers"!

▲ The 185-kilometre Pembrokeshire Coast Path follows the beautiful Pembrokeshire coast.

National Slate Museum

Mount Snowdon

Betws-y-Coed

Beddgelert

Porthmadog

Portmeirion

SNOWDONIA NATIONAL PARK

N
W — E
S

The Snowdon Mountain Railway is a **rack-and-pinion railway**. These trains are made to climb up steep mountains.

From the highest mountain in England and Wales, to a rare flower and mysterious local legends, there is much to discover in Wales' Snowdonia National Park.

Landscape

Snowdonia is famous for its mountain ranges. The highest mountain in England and Wales lies within the park: Mount Snowdon is 1,085 metres tall. Around 350,000 people of all ages climb to its summit each year. It takes around 5–6 hours to climb. But if you're feeling lazy, you can ride the Snowdon Mountain Railway all the way to Snowdon's summit!

Nature

In 1682, the Welsh **botanist** Edward Lhuyd (1660–1709) discovered a very special flower: the Snowdon lily. This pretty plant, with white cup-shaped flowers, has never been seen anywhere else in the UK. It is rare to see this lily in the wild as it only grows on a few bare cliffs high up in the Snowdonia mountains.

▲ Snowdon lily

History

Slate mining was once the biggest industry in north Wales. Slate is a smooth, grey rock used to make roof and floor tiles. Quarrymen dug slate out of huge **quarries**, while miners spent all day underground in slate mines. By the mid-1800s, machines did much of this work. Slate is still an important part of local history. Visitors to the National Slate Museum in Llanberis can tour real slate workshops and watch how slate is split and prepared.

-A legendary dog-

Legend has it that the Prince of Gwynedd owned a faithful dog called Gelert. One day, the Prince returned from hunting to find his baby missing and Gelert with blood around his mouth. Thinking that Gelert had killed the baby, the Prince drew his sword and killed the dog. But then the Prince heard his baby's cries. He also found a dead wolf under the baby's cradle. He quickly realized his mistake – Gelert had saved the baby from the wolf! The Prince buried the brave dog in a grave in Beddgelert, which still stands in the village today.

GLOSSARY

Area of Outstanding Natural Beauty protected area of countryside in England, Wales and Northern Ireland. In Scotland, these areas are called National Scenic Areas.

black market illegal trading of goods

botanist scientist who studies plants, flowers and trees

Bronze Age period in history, after the Stone Age and before the Iron Age, that lasted from around 2500 BC to 800 BC

Catholic member of the Roman Catholic Church

climate change changes in Earth's temperature believed to be caused by pollution

colony community of animals, insects or plants of one kind living close together

conservation protection of landscapes, nature and wildlife

endangered species animal or plant that is seriously at risk of becoming extinct

environmentalist person who tries to protect the environment from damaging human activities

erode gradually wear away

forage hunt or search for food

funicular special type of railway that travels up and down steep slopes

geology scientific study of the rocks of Earth's crust

glacier large body of ice that moves slowly down a slope or valley

herder person who looks after a herd of livestock, such as sheep, cattle or ponies

igneous rock type of rock formed when lava cools

International Dark Sky Reserve special area where very dark skies are protected from light pollution

Iron Age period in history, after the Bronze Age, that lasted from around 800 BC to AD 43

keep tallest and strongest tower in a castle

lichen plant-like fungus that grows on trees, rocks and walls

light pollution man-made light, such as that from cars, streetlamps and homes

limestone type of rock formed over millions of years from marine animal skeletons and shells

migrate move from one area or habitat to another depending on the seasons

peat decaying plant material, similar to soil, which can be dug from the ground and used for fuel

Picts ancient people living in northern Scotland in Roman times

pollution spoiling of the environment due to harmful waste

population number of people living in an area

preserve keep something in its original or existing shape

quarry deep pit where rocks, coal and other types of minerals are dug from the ground

rack-and-pinion railway type of railway that travels up steep mountains

rampart defensive wall of a castle or city

reconstruct build or create something again that has been damaged or destroyed

reed bed area of water or marshland where reeds grow

sandstone type of rock formed over millions of years from layers of sand

spit long, narrow stretch of sand or shingle that extends out to sea

stalactite rock-like structure that hangs from a cave roof, formed by drops of mineral-rich water

stalagmite rock-like structure that rises from a cave floor, formed by drops of mineral-rich water dripping from a cave roof

UNESCO World Heritage Site place recognized by the United Nations as having special educational, scientific or cultural importance

wetland large, wet area of marshes, swamps and bogs

FIND OUT MORE

Websites

There are many great websites for each National Park. You can search for them by going to an internet search engine and typing in the name of the park. Some parks also have free apps, which include maps and other information about the park. Ask your parents to download these apps to their phone or tablet.

Most National Parks also run a Young Rangers programme, where you can be a park ranger for the day! Learn more about how to get involved by typing "Young Rangers" and the park's name into the internet search bar.

combemartinmuseum.co.uk/
Visit this website for dates and times of seashore safaris at Combe Martin beach in Exmoor National Park.

www.dartmoor.gov
See a map showing exactly where wild camping is permitted in Dartmoor National Park.

www.thegreattrossachsforest.co.uk trossachs/great-trossachs-app/
Ask your parents to download the Great Trossachs Forest app for information on walks and landmarks.

▲ Saddle Tor (Dartmoor)

www.nationalparks.gov.uk/
This website will tell you more about every UK National Park.

visitpembrokeshire.com
Find qualified coasteering guides at this Pembrokeshire Coast National Park website.

INDEX